COOL CATS

Siamese

by Rebecca Felix

BLASTOFF! READERS 2

BELLWETHER MEDIA • MINNEAPOLIS, MN

Note to Librarians, Teachers, and Parents:

Blastoff! Readers are carefully developed by literacy experts and combine standards-based content with developmentally appropriate text.

Level 1 provides the most support through repetition of high-frequency words, light text, predictable sentence patterns, and strong visual support.

Level 2 offers early readers a bit more challenge through varied simple sentences, increased text load, and less repetition of high-frequency words.

Level 3 advances early-fluent readers toward fluency through increased text and concept load, less reliance on visuals, longer sentences, and more literary language.

Level 4 builds reading stamina by providing more text per page, increased use of punctuation, greater variation in sentence patterns, and increasingly challenging vocabulary.

Level 5 encourages children to move from "learning to read" to "reading to learn" by providing even more text, varied writing styles, and less familiar topics.

Whichever book is right for your reader, Blastoff! Readers are the perfect books to build confidence and encourage a love of reading that will last a lifetime!

This edition first published in 2016 by Bellwether Media, Inc.

No part of this publication may be reproduced in whole or in part without written permission of the publisher. For information regarding permission, write to Bellwether Media, Inc., Attention: Permissions Department, 5357 Penn Avenue South, Minneapolis, MN 55419.

Library of Congress Cataloging-in-Publication Data

Felix, Rebecca, 1984- author.
  Siamese / by Rebecca Felix.
    pages cm. – (Blastoff! Readers. Cool Cats)
  Summary: "Relevant images match informative text in this introduction to Siamese cats. Intended for students in kindergarten through third grade"– Provided by publisher.
  Audience: Ages 5-8
  Audience: K to grade 3
  Includes bibliographical references and index.
  ISBN 978-1-62617-235-7 (hardcover: alk. paper)
  1. Siamese cat–Juvenile literature. 2. Cat breeds–Juvenile literature. I. Title.
  SF449.S5F45 2016
  636.8'25–dc23
                        2015005955

33614059673987

Table of Contents

What Are Siamese Cats?

Siamese cats are a short-haired **breed**.

They are long and thin
with big eyes and ears.

Siamese cats have
big character, too!

They are one of the most **vocal** cat breeds.

Thailand

N W E S

Siamese cats are among the oldest **domestic** cat breeds. These cats came from Thailand, which used to be called Siam.

Royals and **monks** first owned this breed. In the 1800s, some gave these cats to visiting world leaders.

The President of the United States received one in 1878. It was the first Siamese cat in the country.

Today the Siamese is one of the most popular cat breeds in the world!

Siamese cats have **slender** bodies. They are covered in pale, **silky** fur.

Their long legs and tails have darker fur. These darker areas are called **points**.

The Siamese face and ears also
have points. Point colors can be
seal, chocolate, **lilac**, or blue.

Siamese Coats

seal

chocolate

lilac

blue

Siamese eyes are bright blue. They are **slanted** and almond-shaped.

A long neck holds up a Siamese's narrow head. Large, triangular ears top the head.

Siamese Profile

— large, triangular ears

—— large, blue eyes

———— point coat

Weight: 6 to 14 pounds (3 to 6 kilograms)

Life Span: 11 to 15 years

Siamese cats have a lot of energy. They are playful and **curious**.

They also meow loudly
and often.

Siamese cats need to be **entertained** nearly all the time.

Some people think it is best to own two Siamese cats. That way they always have a playmate!

Glossary

breed—a type of cat

curious—interested or excited to learn or know about something

domestic—animals that are not wild and are kept as pets

entertained—kept busy and interested

lilac—a light gray color

monks—men that live apart from other people because of religious beliefs; monks have many rules that they must follow.

points—areas of darker fur; pointed cats have dark faces, ears, legs, and tails.

royals—kings and queens

seal—very dark brown

silky—soft, smooth, and shiny

slanted—at an angle

slender—thin

vocal—expressing sound often or loudly

To Learn More

AT THE LIBRARY

Owen, Ruth. *Siamese.* New York, N.Y.: PowerKids Press, 2014.

Schachner, Judith Byron. *Skippyjon Jones: Snow What.* New York, N.Y.: Dial-Penguin, 2014.

White, Nancy. *Siamese: Talk to Me!* New York, N.Y.: Bearport Pub., 2011.

ON THE WEB

Learning more about Siamese cats is as easy as 1, 2, 3.

1. Go to www.factsurfer.com.

2. Enter "Siamese cats" into the search box.

3. Click the "Surf" button and you will see a list of related web sites.

With factsurfer.com, finding more information is just a click away.

Index